This Bramcost Publications edition is an unabridged republication
of the rare original work first published in 1952.

www.BramcostPublications.com

ISBN 10: 1-934268-57-7
ISBN 13: 978-1-934268-57-5

Library of Congress Control Number: 2008926735

Bramcost
Publications

It's a frame-up

HAT MAKING SIMPLIFIED

by
IRENE SUTTON

THE "CIRCLE METHOD"

THE "CIRCLE METHOD" Shown are only ten of the possible hundreds of hats, including children's, that can be made from a circle.

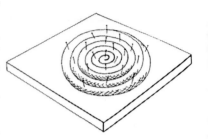

Straw circles can be pushed in, stretched out, pressed flat, drawn up, folded under, turned up, pleated or darted. It can be shaped with a steam iron or by holding the hat over a teakettle. Sizing will hold it firmly in shape. You can shape your hat in your hand while the sizing is drying.

First design and pin your circle to the block. Hold your hat on block over hot steam for a few minutes or press it with a steam iron. Let the straw thoroughly dry. Size to hold the straw in shape. Circle and sew in the hat band. Trim attractively.

Upper left—Cover a canister or jar according to directions in figure 35. Place circle on canister and tie down evenly with ribbon as depth of crown is desired, bringing most fullness to the back. Lightly steam press with an iron to block both top and sides. Pin ribbon to straw all around circle and remove from block. Circle and sew in hat band on inside on the same ribbon line. Now place and pin hat flat on board and press flat except in back. Remove outside ribbon and size. Trim with narrow velvet ribbon and spray of small flowers.

Center left—Stretch and pin lower edge of circle to back of block to get head shape. Bring excess to front by taking a large fold on left side and a smaller fold on lower right side. This gives a completely loose and high brim in front only. Pin to shape. Steam over tea kettle. Thoroughly dry and size. Circle and sew in hat band. Velvet ribbon is around back of crown with two bows tied to a cluster of small roses. Veiling if desired.

Lower left—Shape circle to head block crown in back. The brim is slightly folded down on left side then up slanting to right side. Narrow brim is achieved by folding or pleating brim on crown attractively, bringing in the brim on right side. Steam, size and sew in hat band.

Center right—Place circle forward on block. Pin and press to head shape just enough for shallow crown. Slightly fold and pin up edge a little on each side. Fold back and pin front brim in an attractive line on your head. Steam and dry. Size. Circle and sew in hat band. Cross identical stick-up trimmings in center bringing whips in front outside of brim.

Lower right—Place circle a little forward of block and shape to head size and in a shallow crown leaving brim free to extend out evenly. Fold and pin brim up in back and then down shaping to crown leaving side and end free. Steam, dry, size, and circle and sew in hat band. Place two bows of velvet ribbon in back.

HOW TO MAKE A CIRCLE IN STRAW

It takes four yards of straw braid to make an average circle of 12″ diameter or 5 yards of ¾ inch wide straw. The circle will be smaller or larger according to the amount of straw used. I suggest you use a heavy cardboard, 15″ by 15″, or bread board well covered with tissue paper. You may use your old straw braid hats. First clean the hat with soap and water using a soft brush. Let dry. Unravel the braid and slightly press the braid straight and flat. Your hat can be dyed with hat dye using a brush after the circle is completely shaped, designed and sewed.

Soften the straw braid between a damp cloth as you go along. Start making a center circle as small as possible and underlap and pin to the board each row as you go along. When you have made the circle big enough start bringing the last row under at the outside edge so as not to lose the perfect circle. Interweave the ends into the last row. Hold the board over the steam kettle for a few minutes and let circle thoroughly dry. Start removing the pins at the center back from the board and pin into straw braid enabling you to lift the circle off the board. Sew with a short back stitch, with the thread going between the rows of braid. Don't let the stitches show on either side.

Upper left—Shape, pin and press circle to contour of block in back of circle. Bring fullness of circle to a high fold on left front side of block. Bring fold into pleat, getting smaller as it comes to the right side. Turn up small brim starting at nothing at right side in back and going all around to fold on left side. Steam on block, dry, size, circle and sew in hat band. Stick up trim goes through the large fold in opposite direction—veiling optional.

Upper right—Fabric circle. Cut a 12″ circle of soft buckram or 2 layers of crinoline. Place between two layers of fabric. Sew No. 21 wire on edge of circle with wire stitch (figure 63). Use joiner for ends of wire. Bind with narrow bias strip of same material (figure 58). Bend circle at center back. Fold forward. Take a small pleat across top back. Place two velvet bows on top and inside center back so as to hide any excess folds that are necessary to make circle fit your head. If fabric is heavy, cut out inside where hat fits the head size. Line and sew in hat band.

Center right—Circle is folded down in back and given a little head shape on block by steaming and pressing.

Lower right—Make novelty block of canister (figure 35) about 19″ around and place center of circle slightly forward. Tie with string around on desired depth. Slightly steam. Size crown. Dry. Keeping crown in shape, press brim flat and even. Size and sew in hat band.

Lower left—Circle is centered slightly forward and shaped to head size block. Tie a temporary string around block at desired depth of crown. Dry and size. Now place circle on board and pin and steam press brim flat and even completely around. Size and trim.

A Word About The Author

Women are notorious for their whimsy of buying hats when they are depressed. This could run into an expensive habit, but needn't be. Only perhaps this suggestion would be more agreeable to your budget.

Make your own hats. Besides being an object you can wear with pride you can obtain a lifetime of pleasure and interest from this occupation. This project is something even one with little or no sewing experience will enjoy by following the simple directions in this book.

Have you ever heard the remarks, "I hate hats . . . I never wear hats, they don't do a thing for me! . . . But I must have one for the wedding. Please make me one to go with my dress." No remark could be more foolish. A hat can enhance anyone's looks. It presents a fascinating frame for the face, besides coordinating your attire. If you are an average person with facial shape problems, you can help to overcome these by a carefully selected hat. You wouldn't be so foolish as to insist that you are so lovely or beautiful that you don't need a FRAME-UP. If I will design and make a hat that will do something especially for you, wouldn't you wear it every chance you had? LET A CUSTOM MADE HAT BE YOUR WAY OF SAYING "I'M FASHION-WISE."

I'm of the very definite opinion that fashion is only habit. You can and should wear any hat that is currently in vogue if the lines are adjusted to your features. Even though I'm tall, I've found that a sailor crown can be becoming if the brim is large enough to balance the added height. All styles are not becoming to every one, but you can select one of the new styles and remodel it to your taste. Be fashionable. If you feel a little shy about making a debut with your new hat, wear it around the house until you get used to it. Regardless of how beautiful you looked in your old model, it will look dated now. Don't let people guess your age by your hat. The best way to know what's being worn is to read the articles on the women's pages of your daily newspaper. Watch the pictures in the advertisements. They're always ahead in fashions.

AUTOBIOGRAPHY OF MY MILLINERY EXPERIENCE

One night about ten years ago, I entered an adult education class in dressmaking. The director asked me to fill in at the millinery class. They needed one extra person in order to get the class started. My first reaction was probably like yours—"I'm not an artist in any manner or ability. I can't design hats!" I didn't even know that hats could be made at home. After being in the class one hour, I thought "Why didn't my Mother tell me about this a long time ago!"

ATTEMPTS? MASTERPIECES?

My first HATS were covered frames—no artistic genius needed there. The style and pattern was already decided. Every frame I covered I learned something new. The choice of fabric and trimming was left up to me. Being an average-looking wife of a very handsome man and the mother of five children, I wanted to have attractive, fashionable clothes at the minimum of expense to my husband.

My first hat was a very advanced style frame made from material matching a tailored suit I had just made. Of course I used a casual trimming. The coordination of color, style, type of the suit and hat was the basis of that stylish outfit which was in style for three years. My next hat was a royal blue fabric from a dressmaker suit. Being a flamboyant personality and having a rather long thin face with angular features I placed a pink and deep orchid ribbon and a rose at the back of the brim. The color highlighted my skin tones and drew several favorable comments.

The trimming at the back added softness and width to my face.

Pretty soon I was designing hats without knowing where it all started, and there was a question of whether to sit in the front row in church to concentrate on the services or sitting near the back and watch every hat that proceeded down the aisle.

A millinery shop was my next venture. At the opening I had only three head blocks and a brim board for equipment. This lasted three and a half years. After a while I decided I would rather be home with my family. It was then that I discovered that my customers would come to the house just as easily as to my shop.

After ten years of continuous teaching adult education courses, for Grosse Pointe Woods Community Center, The Neighborhood Club, and the Detroit Board of Education, I now am giving instructions on millinery over TV. These instructions take up, step-by-step, the lessons covered in my book, IT'S A FRAME-UP.

So this is a short summary and an encouragement to you because as you see, I wasn't born with a millinery needle in my hand either.

I would like to dedicate my book to my father, Lawrence Brys, who so wanted me to be a teacher. My son, Clyde, Jr., did the art work.

CONTENTS

IMPORTANT INTRODUCTION

The four basic styles which I am going to present in this booklet will enable you to select any prevailing or desirable style and professionally finish your particular choice *without any other instructions* by applying the step by step directions of the basic styles.

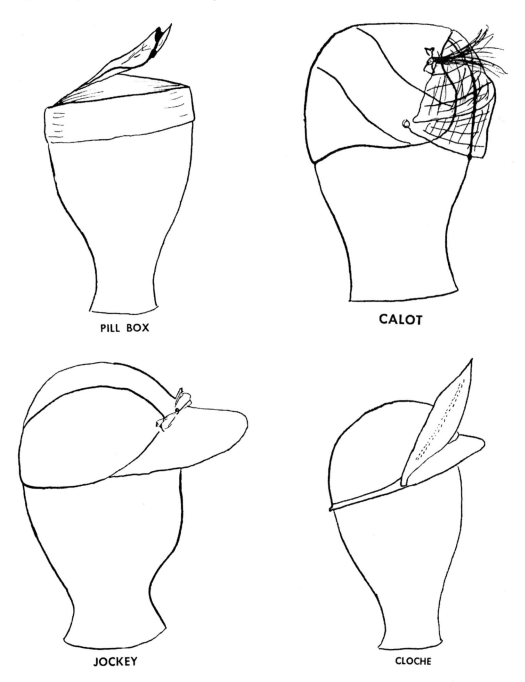

PILL BOX

CALOT

JOCKEY

CLOCHE

SUGGESTIONS

Designing and Draping: Just as soon as you place a personally selected trimming on your hat in a satisfactory position choose a material and start to sew them together on a hat you are a designer. Designing in hat making is a plan, an expression and is an individual dream or desire rather than a paper and pencil drawing.

Draping is nothing more than placing fabric either smoothly or in folds in an attractive position on your hat. *Do not let these two words frighten you.*

Final Steaming: Steaming a hat is the same as pressing a suit; it is the finished touch needed before wearing.

When a hat is completely finished; it should be placed and pinned on the head block in the position you're going to wear it and steamed over the tea kettle. This removes all the wrinkles inside and outside of the hat. It also correctly reshapes your hat to your head size. It also is a good way to refreshen your old hats!

The inside of your hat should be finished as well as the outside.

Don't point out your mistakes to your friends.

Tracing Patterns from Book: Trace all patterns in this book with tissue paper and copy on brown wrapping paper.

Heavy paper may also be used when designing as a substitute for your material.

The pillbox style may be made in any fabric, felt, or straw without a block.

Millinery fabric may be purchased for use in covering frames to match or compliment your clothing; in any weave or color. There are velvets, jerseys, wool, straw cloths or any number of novelty weaves currently popular.

Millinery fabrics are specially woven and treated to lend themselves to easier hatmaking.

Making Individual styled hats: In applying the basic principles to your selection of a hat you might find it necessary to combine instructions of two or more of the basic styles. For example: to make a sailor you would need to copy the pill box directions for the crown and the directions of the cloche for the all around brim. In fabric you would have four separate pieces to put on and use two finish wires and joiners—one on the top crown, and one on the edge of the brim.

Forty thousand yards of dress, coat and suit material sold every week in one of our leading stores in Detroit. Isn't it disturbing to think of the unused material scraps. What about using the left over scraps from your dress, coat or suit to make a hat to match. You could have a custom-made hat for just the cost of a frame. Save yourself $14.95 or more.

A custom-made hat is the epitome of good taste.

HEAD BLOCK

The cost of a head block is usually no more than the price of an inexpensive hat. The *head block is as necessary for hat making as a sewing machine is for dressmaking*. To determine measurement for head block, measure your head by stretching tape firmly from center of forehead around to bump at back of head and back to center of forehead (figure 1). Size will be a 21½, 22, 22½, etc. In marking the head block for individual hair line, start with tape on hair line at center forehead, and measure across head to hair line at nape of neck (figure 2). Draw line on head block following measurement. Start at hair line above left ear, across top of head to hair line above other ear. Draw correspondingly lines on head block. Draw lines connecting four points. This is your true hair line.

If your block is stained use one or two layers of tissue paper over your block to protect the pastel color in your hats.

Pins: Use number 3 super steel pins for millinery. These are longer and stronger than other pins. Because of the curves in hats all pinning should be done vertically for best results.

Needles: Use No. 7 millinery needles for easier sewing on hats. Millinery needles are longer, thinner, and have a sharper point than regular sewing needles. Sizes No. 4 to No. 10 (No. 4 is the larger, thicker one, as the number increases, etc.).

Thread: Use special milliner's thread —glazed No. 50 preferred. This thread is stronger, does not knot easily and looks better because of the glazed finish. You can glaze cotton thread by rubbing it between 2 pieces of wax.

HOW TO MEASURE YOUR HEAD FOR A HEAD BLOCK

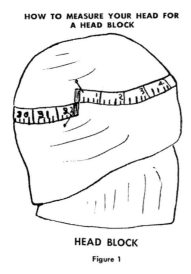

HEAD BLOCK

Figure 1

In order to make a head block larger steam and stretch an old felt over the head block; this method will make your block one half inch bigger.

HOW TO MARK YOUR HEAD BLOCK

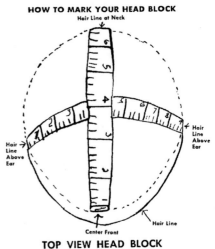

TOP VIEW HEAD BLOCK

Figure 2

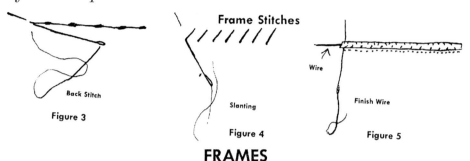

Frame Stitches

Back Stitch

Figure 3

Slanting

Figure 4

Wire

Finish Wire

Figure 5

FRAMES

A buckram frame is the pattern and foundation for the type and style of hat you are going to make. The buckram frame itself is usually constructed from buckram, wire, crinoline, and sometimes flexo, shaped to a definite style and head size. The buckram frames serve as a base (the same as a pattern in dress making) for the fabric covering. Any material that is generally acceptable for clothing can be used. The amount of material needed will be governed by the size of the frame to be covered. Scraps may be sewed together in a pattern. It is *essential to always cut on the bias,* so that the material will stretch sufficiently to follow the contour of the frame.

How to Adjust Frames: To make a frame smaller, unravel thread and remove crinoline on center back. Locate where wire overlaps. Slit buckram frame, *never wire,* from bottom of frame to center of crown. Overlap buckram until it is small enough for desired head size (figure 6). Place frame over head block and press out any bumps with iron, using slightly dampened cloth. Don't fold wire but slip back up into frame. Wire will extend further around bottom of frame. If large adjustment is made, cut same amount off *ends* of wire. To make larger (figure 7), open dart and sew by basting in extra piece of buckram. Sew wire back in place, then also sew crinoline in place.

PAPER PATTERNS are usually taken from flat or only slightly curved surfaces, flat crowns, or brims. *Material can be easier draped over some crowns and some brims.* It is a good idea to know how to take a paper pattern because you can

apply the same principle when copying another hat.

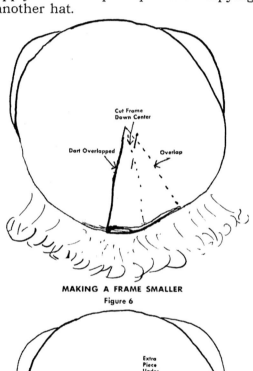

Cut Frame Down Center

Dart Overlapped

Overlap

MAKING A FRAME SMALLER
Figure 6

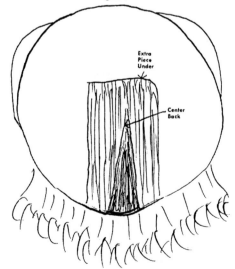

Extra Piece Under

Center Back

MAKING A FRAME LARGER
Figure 7

PAPER PATTERN DIRECTIONS

PILLBOX: The *paper pattern* is made of tissue paper or newspaper. Start with the crown by placing paper over frame (figure 8). If the crown has any curves, fold the excess paper into a dart, (as in dressmaking) slash dart down center to point, overlap and vertically pin to frame. (All pinning that is done on the frame should be vertical for best results.) *Make as many darts as are necessary to enable the paper pattern to closely fit the crown.* Cut excess paper off edge of crown. Pencil mark center front, (C. F.) center back, (C. B.) left and right sides.

For the side crown place paper around side crown. Slash, overlap, and vertically pin to frame making paper follow shape of side crown all around. Cut off top and bottom *true* to *frame*—never allow for seams in a paper pattern. Pencil mark C. B., C. F., left and right sides, and top and bottom. Slash through center back of pattern for seam. Carefully lift pattern from frame by removing pins and replacing on paper, without disturbing shape of paper.

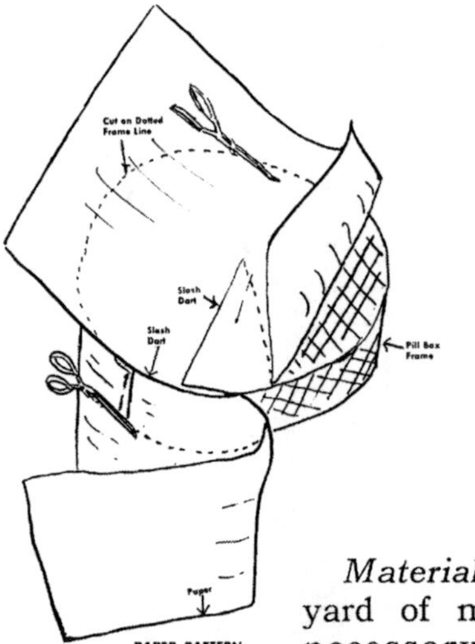

PAPER PATTERN
Figure 8

Material: Only 1/3 yard of material is necessary for most hats because it makes cutting on the bias possible. The pillbox frame requires 2/3 yard, but with careful planning of seams, less

material may be used. Instead of placing one seam down center back, two seams equally placed on the right and left side making a design, may be used. *The general rule for seams is follow the lines on frame.* The pillbox has a definite line on the top of side crown. Therefore the pillbox style will be made in two pieces. Where crown meets brim, and where brim is in two sides—top and bottom or inside and outside. Also, whenever a wire is controlling the style line of the frame. *A No. 21 milliner's wire is used whenever two pieces of material are to be sewed together, regardless of the wire in the frame that controls the design line.*

Padding Frames: When the material is so thin that you can see the frame through you need to pad the frame with sheet wadding. Sheet wadding comes in squares of 36 inches by 27 inches. It's the thin cotton padding used in making shoulder pads. If you pad your frame too thick it gives it a heavy look. Separate the padding into two thin layers. Using ½ thickness with the fuzzy side next to frame. Smoothly drape over the frames, any extra thickness or fold that form should be cut right out and the raw edges just meet. (As a dart in dressmaking you would cut right out on the stitching line and bring the raw edges of the padding together.) Never *overlap* padding; only slightly baste the padding to the frame so as *not* to *form* a heavy seam (figure 9).

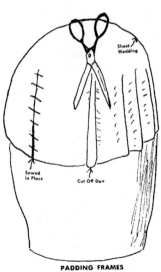

PADDING FRAMES
Figure 9

CUTTING AND PLACING MATERIAL ON FRAMES

To cut material place paper pattern of crown and brim on true bias of material (figure 10). Allow ½ inch for seams.

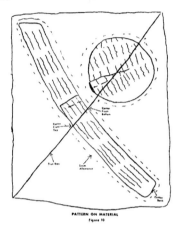

PATTERN ON MATERIAL
Figure 10

Transfer the markings from the paper pattern to the material with tailor's chalk. When placing the fabric on the frame match corresponding positions, i.e., center front of material to center back of material to center back of frame etc. Stretch smoothly and vertically pin material over crown ¼ inch coming down to side crown. (Figure 11). Sew closely to top of side crown using back stitch. Cut off excess seam allowance. Place and pin material on side crown, matching positions as before. Bring and pin bottom of material over and under to inside of frame. There should be at least ½ inch seam allowance inside of

bottom crown. Before sewing bottom it is necessary to pin top of side crown in place. For top of side crown a number 21 (figure 14) finishing wire is needed to control the bias and add a professional finish. *(Regardless of the wire already in the frame.)* Use exactly enough wire to go around edge of the topside of crown. Starting with center back of crown (figure 12), place material over

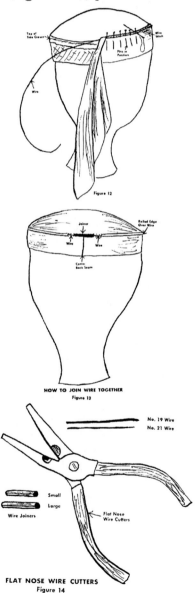

Figure 12

HOW TO JOIN WIRE TOGETHER
Figure 13

No. 19 Wire
No. 21 Wire

Small
Large
Wire Joiners
Flat Nose
Wire Cutters

FLAT NOSE WIRE CUTTERS
Figure 14

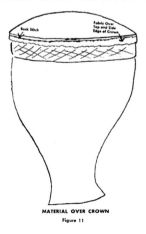

MATERIAL OVER CROWN
Figure 11

wire and pin vertically so that wire forms an *edge on line of crown, never below or never above crown figure line.* This wire finishing method is much like a cording in slip-covers. The wire can be basted in position before the material is placed on the hat. You must either pin the wire tightly as a cording or baste closely along wire as if the wire is the cord. In pinning be sure fabric is pulled up tightly from bottom. Success will be in placing the pins vertically, just below the wire and through the frame. Continue in this manner to center back. To prevent the wires from protruding and tearing material use joiners (figure 14), or connectors (figure 13). Insert ends of wire in joiner and pinch tightly with pliers. A flat-nosed wire cutter is preferred. This tool is handy for cutting wire and tightening joiners. Sew inside bottom first, use slanting stitch, being careful not to let any stitching show on the outside of hat. The top side of crown is sewed with a wire finishing stitch.

Finish Wire Stitch: The finish wire stitch is used where two pieces of material are to be sewed together, such as top of crown to side crown, and on a brim edge. It helps to form a straight line and controls the bias; thereby giving a professional finish. *Slip stitching or machine stitching pieces of fabric together without wire gives a homemade appearance.* A controlled wire line is also used in designing. In other words a wire finish can be used anywhere on a hat if it follows a pattern of design. Remember a wire should either be fastened together by a joiner or be brought around the hat and under and inside the crown when ended. If you end it abruptly on the crown or brim, the sharp end will tear and work through the material.

Starting at center back or beginning of wire from top, bring needle and thread under wire and through material to outside. (Knot is hidden between frame and material.) Then start back approximately 1/16 of an inch from last stitch; place needle *closely* under wire and

through fabric lightly catching top of crown material. Do not sew through frame. Keep thread pulled tightly. *Do not catch top crown of material going back;* go directly under wire to outside coming out at the end of last stitch. This outside finish stitch should give the effect of one continuous stitch below the tightly covered fabric wire. Continue around to beginning or end of wire.

LINING: Milliners use size georgette or French crepe because once it is blocked it will *retain* its shape and *will not need to be sewed to the top of the frame.* Home sewers use organdy or taffeta, preferably organdy. *Never* use coat or suit lining material. A lining is used in a frame to protect your hair and to cover all the seams and rough edges of the material. It is not necessary to have the lining fit way up into the crown, but just enough to cover your head, yet high enough to keep the frame from sitting on top of your head.

Choose one of the four basic colors for lining and hat banding (Black, Navy, Brown, White). Dark colors show less soil.

Lining: Use 12 inch square of lining fabric (either organdy, French crepe, or taffeta) place corners diagonal-wise (figure 15), one point at center back and the other at center front of block. Remaining two points should be one over each ear, or on the sides. Steam on block. Firmly pin and stretch material to block, running pins upward (figure 16). Hold block in both hands over steam of tea kettle, pull tightly and stretch while damp (figure 17). Use several pins pinning upward, *steaming* as you go along, until all wrinkles have been removed. Let dry 15 minutes. Mark C. B. and C. F. Carefully lift off head block and place inside crown of hat in correct position (figure 18). Pin to top of hat. Lining must fit loosely otherwise it will hold hat off head. Pin and sew to fabric — use slanting stitch (without hemming). Cut off excess lining ¼" below bottom of frame.

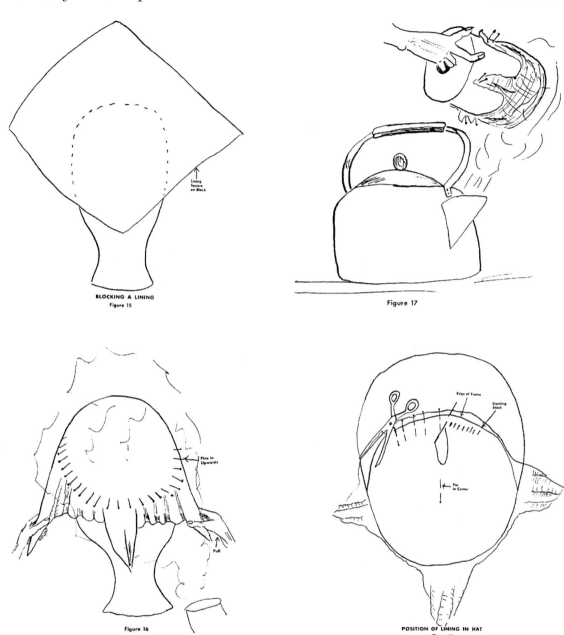

BLOCKING A LINING
Figure 15

Figure 17

Figure 16

POSITION OF LINING IN HAT
Figure 18

A crown shaped lining may be used in any hat, but if there is no head block available make a tailored lining as follows: Using paper pattern cut lining material on true bias, allowing ¼ inch for seams. Sew top crown to top side of crown either by machine or by hand, on wrong side of material. Press open seams between fingers. Place lining inside of hat, wrong side next to frame. Do *not turn* bottom under as a hem. Lining must fit well into crown. Stitch lightly around bottom of lining. Cut off excess seam allowance.

HAT BAND: Although hat banding resembles grosgrain ribbon, it does not have threads running along edge. Hat banding ribbon has a saw tooth edge, without threads, which makes stretching and shrinking possible. Measure ribbon hat banding around bottom of pillbox frame, allowing one inch for shrinkage and one inch for turning under seam at center back (figure 19). Place hat banding on ironing board under wet

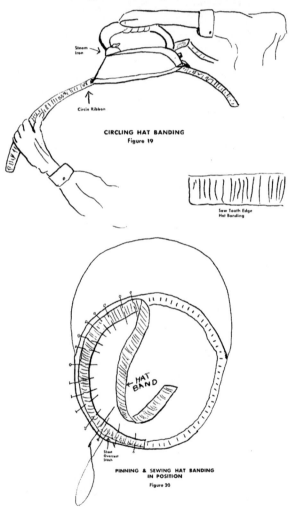

Steam Iron

Circle Ribbon

CIRCLING HAT BANDING
Figure 19

Saw Tooth Edge
Hat Banding

HAT BAND

Short Overcast Stitch

PINNING & SEWING HAT BANDING IN POSITION
Figure 20

pressing cloth, go over one lightly with iron, remove cloth and with iron directly on ribbon, shape into a semicircle. It is not necessary to use a wet cloth if you have a steam iron. Place and vertically pin outside circle of hat banding ¼ inch

below inside edge of frame, beginning at center back and ending by folding the banding back one inch at center back. The inside of the semicircle always goes towards top of the hat to correspond with the contour of the head. Sew to fabric, using short overcasting stitches. (Figure 20).

Trimmings: Feather pattern, (figure 21), trace and cut two on true bias of material and two on bias of interfacing or crinoline. Place nine inch wire, either use No. 21 wire, pipe cleaner, or picture wire, between the two pieces of interfacing. One feather of material goes on top and the other on bottom. Machine top stitch through material and interfacing; stitching completely around wire starting at bottom of feather. Next stitch three rows around unhemmed edge. Give feather a slight twist between fingers for dash and softness. Pin and tack on at an attractive angle.

For tubing (figure 22), cut on yard strip of bias, 1½ inch wide, piecing if necessary. Fold down center. Machine stitch ½ inch from fold. Don't cut off seam allowance, reverse tubing. (String one yard upholstery cording through sewed strip, optional.) Also insert one yard of number 20 wire and sew the ends of tubing

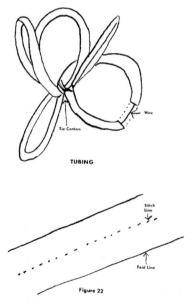

Wire

Tie Centers

TUBING

Stitch Line

Fold Line

Figure 22

closed. The wire holds tubing stiff. Wind
tubing around four fingers until entire
amount is taken up, sew and fasten ends
of tubing together and tie bottom of
circles together. Place and sew on hat in
an attractive position. Give each circle a
half twist to give softness.

Veilings: Veilings are usually put on
hats to flatter and soften the lines of a
hat, like frosting on a cake. One yard of
veiling is usually sufficient. Place hat
on your head. Drape veiling across face
in position you desire over face. Pin
center of veiling to center of hat. Gather
veiling at bottom side with both hands,
grasping veiling and working towards
center top, forming a basket over the
face. Pin same on other side. Drape
excess veiling on crown of hat. Veiling
may also be wrapped and folded around
the hat. Never over sew, merely tack.

Covered and felt hat pins: Hat pins are
a necessity, also are an added detail, if
made of the same material as the hat.
To make, cut out a foundation of felt or
buckram (figures 23-24), any shape may
be used, circle, diamond, square, rec-
tangle, etc. Cut large enough to cover
hat pin. Using foundation, cut one on
material allowing ¼ inch all around
for seam. Fold fabric over felt and turn
seam allowance inside. Fold in half over
head of pin and overcast completely
around head of hat pin.

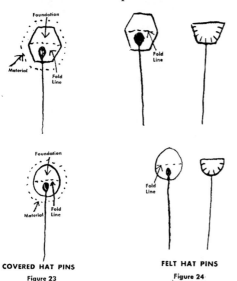

COVERED HAT PINS
Figure 23

FELT HAT PINS
Figure 24

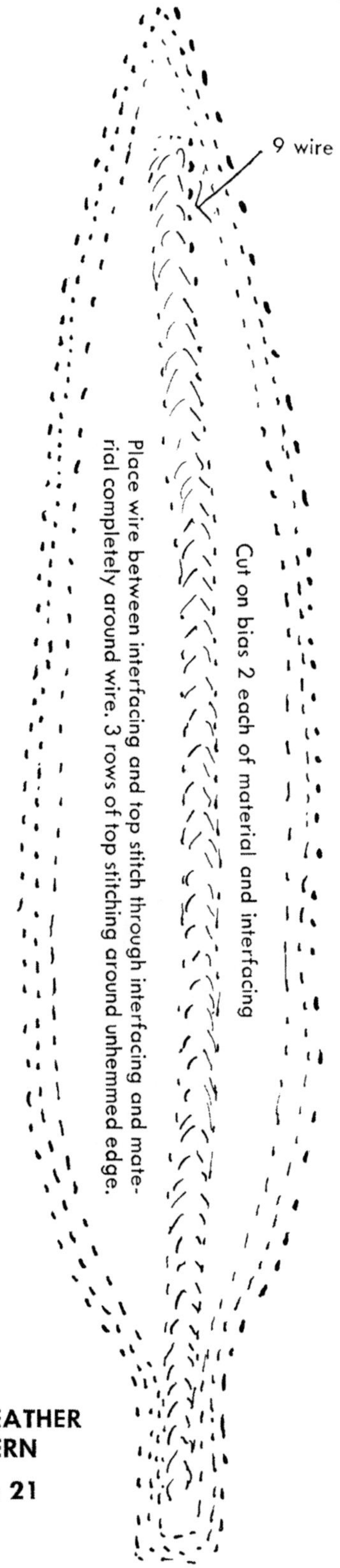

9 wire

Place wire between interfacing and top stitch through interfacing and material completely around wire. 3 rows of top stitching around unhemmed edge.

Cut on bias 2 each of material and interfacing

**FABRIC FEATHER
PATTERN**
Figure 21

Finish: All hats before ready to wear, must be put on head block and steamed. This steaming takes out all little wrinkles and presses hat. Allow hat to dry on head block, and it is ready to wear.

CALOT or BEANIE: The *one piece crown* is used when material is loosely woven and calot is not too deep; this is the simpler method. At least a 12 inch square of material is necessary to make a one piece crown. See pictures for blocking square of lining. Use the same method (figures 15, 16, 17). Pin square over block, placing one point at center back bottom and opposite point center back bottom. Each of two remaining points cover ear. Firmly pin and stitch material to block running pins upward. Hold block in both hands and place over steam of tea kettle tightly stretching and closely pinning material upward, steaming as you go along until all wrinkles in fabric have been removed. It is only necessary to remove wrinkles as far down as crown is going to be. Dry thoroughly, mark center back and center front. Carefully lift off fabric from block without stretching. Place and match positions on frame. Bring material over edge and to inside of frame ¼ inch and pin vertically. Fabric should fit *smoothly* over frame. Sew fabric to frame with stitch slanting (figure 4), being careful not to let stitches show through on outside.

Sectional crown: This method is used when a design in the crown is desired. Also when you only have small pieces to work with. The sectional crown minimizes a large head size. Place *calot frame* in correct position on head block. Place material on true bias on center of frame and cut off desired piece (figure 25). Or measure calot center front diagonally to center back. Using this measurement, adding two inches for seams, on each end. Cut fabric 3½ inches wide

on true bias. Center and pin fabric to crown.

Side: Use three cornered piece of material, large enough to cover one side of crown, pin true bias to bottom edge of frame (figure 26). Now fit smoothly and pin top remaining fabric along stitch line on center piece. *Never vary seam allowance on center strip.* The width of center piece of material should always remain the same. Cut away excess seam allowance on side piece. Chalk mark line along both sides of pins for sewing guide line. Follow same procedure for other side. Carefully lift on frame. Baste on chalk line. Machine stitch slightly stretching fabric as you go along. Place fabric crown *on block* without frame in correct position, wrong side up (figure 27). Stretching and pinning, steam out all wrinkles. Keep seam lines in a straight line on block. To steam, hold over tea kettle and stretch material down. Steam seams open and flat. Allow to dry thoroughly. Loosely baste seams down *temporarily* ¼ inch from each side of seams. Stretch and pull material smoothly in proper position over frame, over and under ¼ inch inside of frame. Sew with slanting stitch (figure 4).

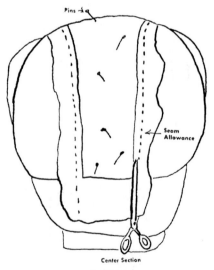

Pins

Seam Allowance

Center Section

Sectional crown
Figure 25

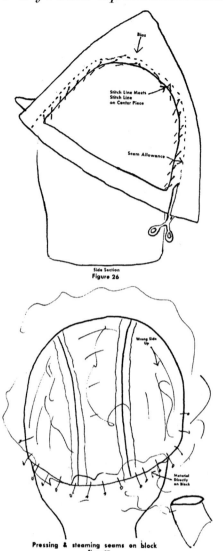

Side Section
Figure 26

The cockade trim, use 1½ yards of hat band ribbon (figure 28). Begin at one end and make ⅛ inch pleat across ribbon, press with fingers. Stitch inside bottom edge of pleat. Make another ⅛ inch pleat, just below and tack to first. Continue, use all of ribbon tacking each pleat with one continual thread. This will form a string of pleats which can be twisted and turned into any stunning arrangement. Place on hat, tacking loosely.

Veiling: Besides being appealing, veiling is put on the calot to add width and give the illusion of "more hat." (See pillbox veiling.)

COCKADE TRIM

Figure 28

Pressing & steaming seams on block
Figure 27

Although lines of calot are parallel (front to back) center can be cut on bias strip from side to side. The side pieces would be one front and one back. Also, if only small pieces are available, any pattern may be arranged by drawing lines on the frame and matching material to them.

Lining: Block and sew in lining. Follow instructions under Lining.

Trimming: Circle and sew in hat banding. Tubing or cockade ribbon makes an attractive trimming. The calot is an extremely dressy hat and commercial trimming is its best asset.

JOCKEY: The *crown* can be made in the same manner as the calot (figures 25-26-27). In using the sectional crown the seam lines go from front to back. A pie shaped design may also be used. When finished crown fabric is placed over frame turn material over and under ¼ inch at back beginning of brim. On each side, pin and backstitch unhemmed edge on line where brim meets crown.

The brim paper pattern is made according to past directions under pillbox (figure 8). Cut two of material on true bias (top and bottom) allow for seams. Pin top piece in position on brim. Turn under ¼ inch edge where brim meets crown and blind stitch to crown fabric. Bring outside edge over and under edge of frame ¼ inch (figure 29). Sew to frame with slanting stitch. Place bottom piece of brim material in position. Bring inside brim seam allowance inside of crown and pin. On outside edge of brim fold seam allowance over number 21 wire and pin in position to edge of frame. Use enough wire to reach from one edge of brim to the other, plus two inches. Covered wire must come to very edge, not below, over, or above brim. Sew with finish wire stitch (figure 5). Pin and sew wire to end of brim and turn back wire ½ inch, inside of crown. Press wire with snub-nosed clippers and sew to frame. This eliminates the possibility of the wire sticking through the frame or picking the head. Put in lining according to pillbox directions. Circle and sew in hat banding (figure 22).

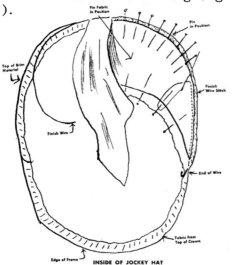

INSIDE OF JOCKEY HAT
Figure 29

Trimming: Tubing of the same material can be used, by tying the tubing in a bow and place at center front. Also a ribbon may be used. Take two pieces of ribbon measuring ½ yard and tack at each end of brim, tying bow in the center of brim.

CLOCHE: The crown is made in either one piece (if enough material is at hand) (figures 15-16-17), or in a sectional design following the instructions for the calot (figures 25-26-27). _Except_ for placing the material over the frame. Smooth the material over frame and pin the line where the brim meets the crown. Backstitch (figure 3).

The brim: Make a paper pattern (figures 8 and 11) or loosely drape material across the bottom brim, allowing for seams. Cut two; one for the top and one for the bottom. If paper pattern method is used make seam in center of pattern back (figure 10). Pin and place top piece of material to lines of frame on brim, center front to center back, etc. Slash horizontally inside seams allowance if covering is too tight. If frame is concave on either top or bottom, lightly spread glue on _frame_ and press material with hands. Glue _must be partially dry._ When it is too thick it has a tendency to show through the material and cannot be removed. Temporarily baste where material is glued. This will hold material to curve until hat is completed. Use milliners or adhesive glue for quick drying. Bring material over bottom edge of frame to ¼ inch below and sew using slanting stitch (figure 29). Turn under seam allowance inside brim where it meets the crown. Sew with slip stitch. Place and pin bottom of brim fabric in position according to marking. On outside edge of brim fold seam allowance over number 21 wire and pin in position to edge of frame (figure 29). Covered wire must come to very edge, not below, over or above brim. Pin and sew to top of fabric using finish wire stitch (figure 5). Use joiner to hold wire together in center back (figure 13). Block and sew in lining (figures 15-16-17-18). Circle and sew in hat banding (figure 19).

Trimming: For casual trim use feather or cockade ribbon, usually place on right side. Ribbon hat banding may be tied around crown, as a trimming but remember to shrink and circle first before placing on hat. See instructions for hat banding (figure 19). A veil and/or flowers are used for a more dressy hat.

DRAPING FABRICS IN RELATION TO FRAMES

Materials can be draped on any frame in many different folds, always working in a pattern of your own design. Steam and block a ten inch square of any suitable fabric over a block according to directions for a one piece crown (figures 15-16-17). Lift off material from block and place over calot frame in proper position on block. Material need not cover frame entirely (figure 30). Pin in position. Using a true bias strip of material approximately five inches wide and ¾ yard long (amount of material necessarily can be determined by what is available). Working with frame on head block, pin one corner of material to center front of frame (figure 30). Take material in hand and *firmly stretch,* wrapping, folding, and pleating as you progress around the block. Material must cover bottom of frame. Pin in position as you stretch. Material will drape in an attractive manner if you let the folds follow the contour of the hat. Grasp remaining material and fold into a bow, knot or draped around a rose (figure 31), stretching and pinning to frame as you go along. Take block in both hands and thoroughly steam draped fabric over the tea kettle. THIS PROCESS WILL PERMANENTLY SET ANY PLEATS, FOLDS, OR DRAPES IN THE FABRIC. Thoroughly dry on block. To sew, raise up folds and take small stitching under fold, going continuously from fold to fold, with one long thread tacking wherever necessary. Bring bottom fold under frame and sew with slanting stitch. Put in lining and hat band. If a bow is desired, start and end on a side instead of center front. Give hat a final steaming on block.

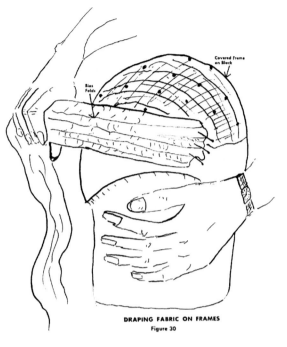

DRAPING FABRIC ON FRAMES
Figure 30

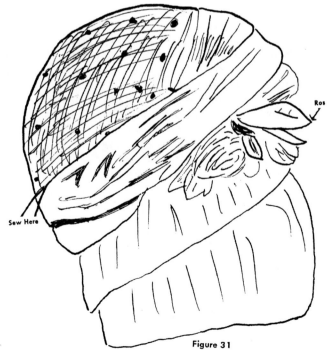

Figure 31

FELTS

A felt hat is what milliners term a "soft hat". The design is carried out in the cutting and draping of the felt, to suit individual features. THE SHAPE OF A FELT CAN BE COMPLETELY CHANGED BY STEAMING AND STRETCHING OVER A BLOCK. Wool felts are very inexpensive, which harden and become stiff in the blocking process. This type of felt is good to use for practice. Fur felts make quality hats and are especially ideal for those interested in designing. They are soft, pliable, and drape easily. A felt hood and body may be purchased according to the type of hat to be made (figure 34). For a small hat use a hood and for a large hat especially one with a brim use a felt body.

Novelty blocks: Assuming that a head block is not available for the pillbox style, we suggest using an article which measures 6½ to 8 inches in diameter, possibly a sugar cannister (figure 35). For a hat of another style anything which suggests a crown, may be used; a small wooden salad bowl without legs for a beret (figure 37), a pointed tomato juice strainer for a pixie (figure 36), a kettle cover or plate for a round flat crown. A felt is blocked on the novelty block *first,* then placed and steamed on your head block for head size.

Before the novelty block is ready for use it must be covered with cloth so as to have something to stick pins in. To cover, use two inch wide strips of material from an old sheet long enough to

Felt Stitches

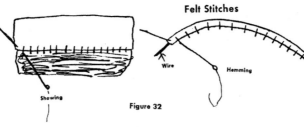

Figure 32

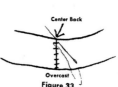

Figure 33

Restyling: To gain daring and confidence use an old felt hat, preferably fur felt. Remove trimmings, ribbons, wire, hat band, and stitching from old hat; also separate brim from crown if they are made in two pieces. Temporarily sew by hand together any holes otherwise the holes will get larger in the blocking process. Thoroughly clean dark felts with dry cleaning fluid. Pastel felts may be *hand washed* with a gentle action soap. Place and pin wet felt over head block until dry. Rub over lightly with sand paper after hats are completely finished.

Felts may be home dyed just like cloth or any article of clothing.

Freshly cut edges of felt should be rubbed between two pieces of sand paper.

Linings are *not necessary* in felt hats.

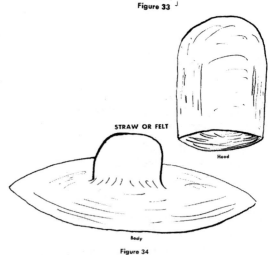

STRAW OR FELT

Figure 34

reach the center bottom of the sugar cannister (figure 35). Start at center bottom of cannister go up and across to the other side. Either sew or pin ends together at top and bottom of cannister.

Continue to follow this process until the cannister is completely covered by 2 inch strips of cloth. The pillbox block is complete and ready to use. Place thoroughly cleaned old felt hat over spout of steaming tea kettle until the felt becomes damp (figure 38). Covered with pearls of steam. This takes about three minutes. Quickly place felt over cloth covered sugar cannister. Stretch and pull out all wrinkles, pinning and steaming as you go along (figure 38). This keeps the felt from returning to its orginal shape. Place pins three inches from the top, always stretching felt down. Let dry about two hours. Drying time may be shortened by pressing the hat on the block with an iron over a damp cloth. *Pressing with iron and a wet cloth stiffens felt.* Never place iron directly on felt, always use a pressing cloth. Chalk mark 2¼ inches or any desired width from top all around. Fold under on chalk line. Lightly press hat on edge of fold line. Remove from block

Circle and sew in hat band (figures 19-20).

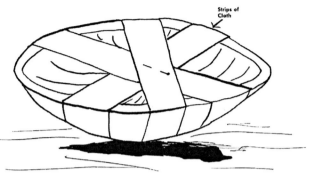

SALAD BOWL
Figure 37

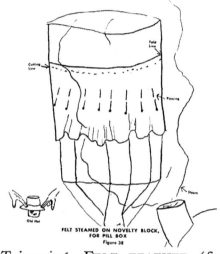

FELT STEAMED ON NOVELTY BLOCK,
FOR PILL BOX
Figure 38

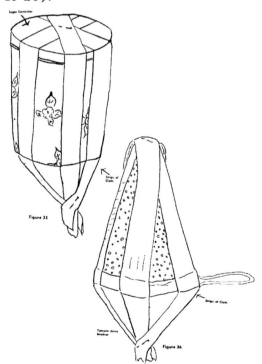

Figure 35

Figure 36

Trimming: FELT FEATHER (figure 39). Press excess felt flat and smooth. Trace pattern with tissue paper and chalk mark on felt. Use No. 21 wire about 9 inches long. Hem felt on one side of feather over wire starting ½ inch from bottom going within ½ inch of tip. Use hemming stitch (figure 32), being careful to not show stitch on wrong side. Evenly slash on an angle in ¾ of an inch starting at top and going down to end of feather. When finished give the feather an attractive twist. Two feathers are suggested for the pill box. Place feather starting at center back with the tips meeting in the front. For all around fringed feather, slash felt on angle on both side. Fold felt over wire running down the center (figure 40). Closely machine sew with cording foot or by hand. Press feather open between fingers. To finish feather give a slight twist.

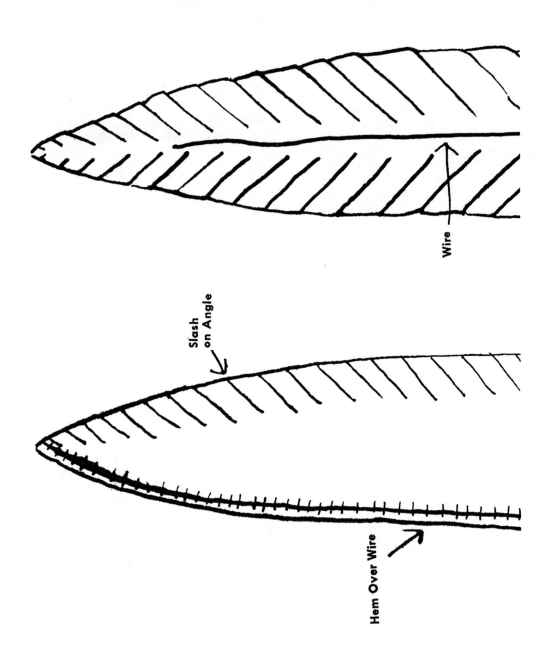

FELT FEATHER PATTERN

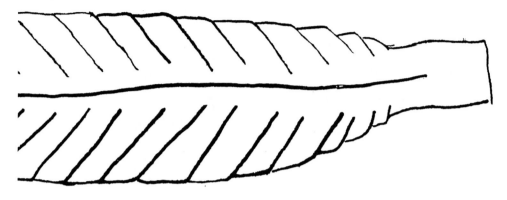

Figure 40

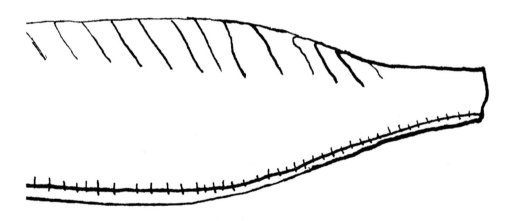

Figure 39

FELT FEATHER PATTERN

Orchid. Cut orchid pattern according to directions (figure 41). Place No. 21 wire starting one inch below top of petals Nos. 1, 2. Fold felt over wire, hand stitch closely along wire with invisible stitch or machine stitch with cording foot. Group fronds together according to real orchid (figure 42). Sew securely to hat at a becoming angle.

Veiling: Drape veiling over front of pillbox to give a soft, feminine look. This also adds width to the pillbox.

Hat pins: Cut out any desired shape (figure 24). Place hat pin in the center, start at top and overcast around open edges.

ORCHID
Figure 42

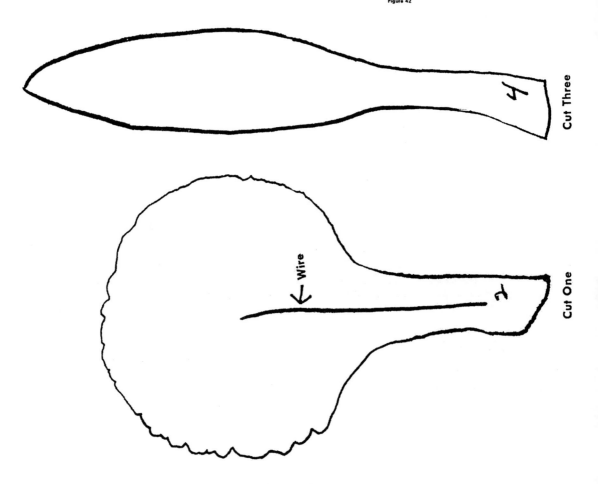

ORCHID PATTERN

Figure 41

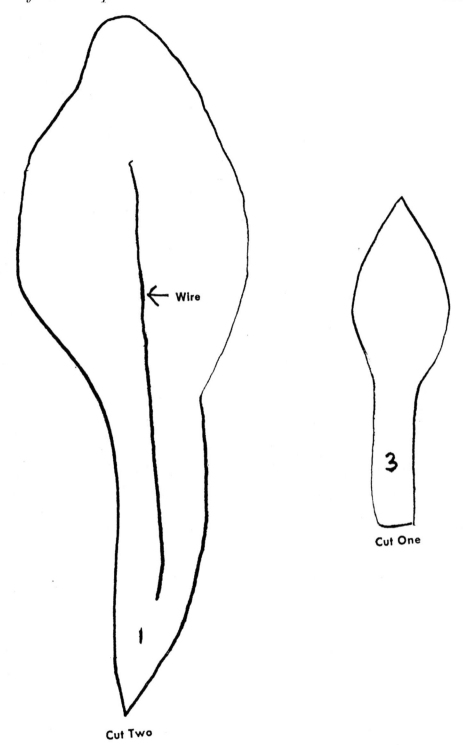

ORCHID PATTERN
Figure 41

SAILOR HAT

To make a sailor hat you would block and steam your hat on the novelty block; cannister or something with an oval or round shape; in the same manner as the pill box crown, turning under at the desired height of crown. To make the brim you would press the felt, *smoothly,* flat (figure 53), and form a collar around the same novelty block instead of your own block, as the crown was blocked on; that is to make the brim and crown the same head size. Cut the width of brim to suit your features; the crown fits over the collar of the brim. Join the brim with straight seam center back using overcasting stitch. Hem brim over wire if necessary to hold design line.

For the following hats a head block is necessary. Use previous instructions for measurements, etc.

CALOT: Place old hat or new hood over steaming spout of tea kettle long enough to thoroughly dampen felt (figure 43). Quickly place on head block in position calot will be worn (figure 44-45). Pull and stretch out all the wrinkles below hair line. *Using measurement for your hair line (figure 2) that you marked on block. Chalk mark hair line on felt* (figure 26). Mark out design with chalk for scalloped calot (figure 46), cut out calot, or one-sided calot, according to your hair line. Cut

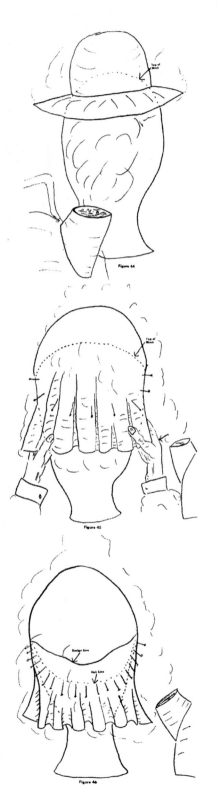

Figure 44

Figure 45

Figure 46

STEAMING & BLOCKING FELTS

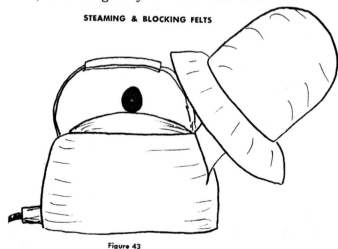

Figure 43

away excess felt of ½ inch below design line. Turn under on design line and press edge with damp cloth and iron very lightly.

Circle and sew in hat banding (figures 19-20).

Trimming: Felt rose. Press out long narrow strip of left over felt. At three inch intervals (figure 47), starting at bottom with single basting thread, baste on angle to top and down to bottom again. Draw up until slightly gathered, tie knot on bottom. On bottom edge gather with double thread. Roll felt until rose is formed.

Veiling is optional. Steam for final finish.

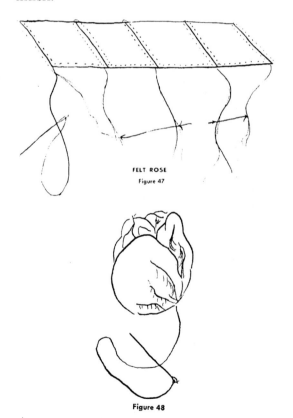

FELT ROSE
Figure 47

Figure 48

JOCKEY: Steam old hat or new felt body over tea kettle and place on block (figures 43-44-45-46). Pull and stretch felt in the same manner as calot, removing all wrinkles above hair line. Thoroughly dry. *Mark hair line on felt.*

Cut ½ inch below hair line, cutting off excess material. No special design is needed in a jockey style. Try on for fit. The jockey should fit comfortably just above ears and dip in back about one inch above hair line. Mark with chalk any adjustments, and fold up at desired depth. Place back on block and cut ½ inch below any new design or fitting line. Fold under and press on edge. Press out wrinkles of left over piece of felt on ironing board, keeping felt in a circle as much as possible (figure 52). Make a paper pattern of brim from given visor pattern (figure 49). Adjust pattern to features, if necessary make smaller by cutting outside of line of brim (The brim is rarely made larger). You can stretch and fit felt to the size of the pattern by steam pressing with iron and pulling brim to desired shape, pin down to ironing board till dry allowing ½ inch inside of brim and ¼ inch around outside for seams. Trace visor pattern with chalk and cut out. Hem ¼ inch seam allowance over wire, No. 19, using hemming stitch (figure 32) don't go through felt. Wire should be sufficiently long enough to go around outside of the brim. Let wire extend out ½ inch at each end. Clip and turn up seam allowance inside circle of brim against bottom of block to form a collar (figure 53). Place brim collar inside of hat under crown. Pin and sew in position from inside, stitches shouldn't show through.

Circle and sew in hat band. Give felt hat a final steaming and allow to dry.

Trimming: A thin well pressed strip of felt, ¼ inch wide, can be tacked from left side of brim to right making a felt bow in the center (figure 50). *Felt bow.* Use narrow strip of felt generally ¼ inch in width and 24 inches long. Cut ends diagonally. Fold in half, make loop on one side, using all except enough to extend for a tail. Fold over at center. Using same proportions make other side of bow. Secure in center of bow. Cut narrow strip, ½ inch by ¼ inch,

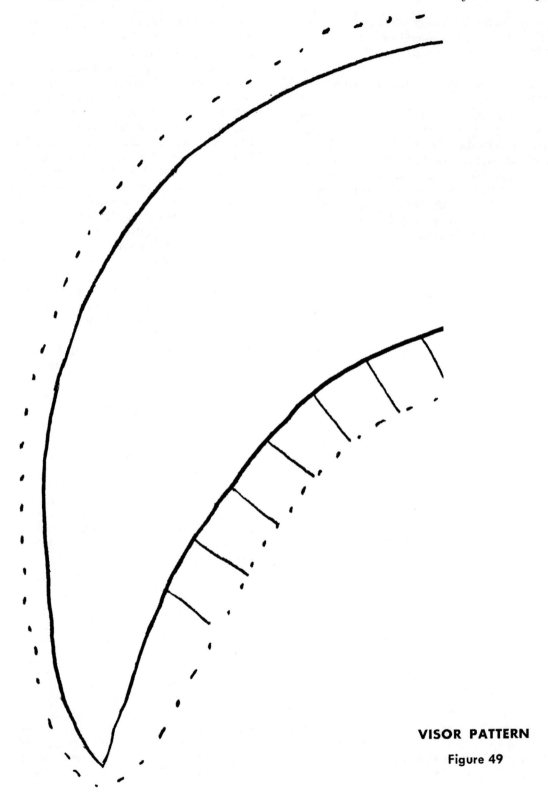

VISOR PATTERN

Figure 49

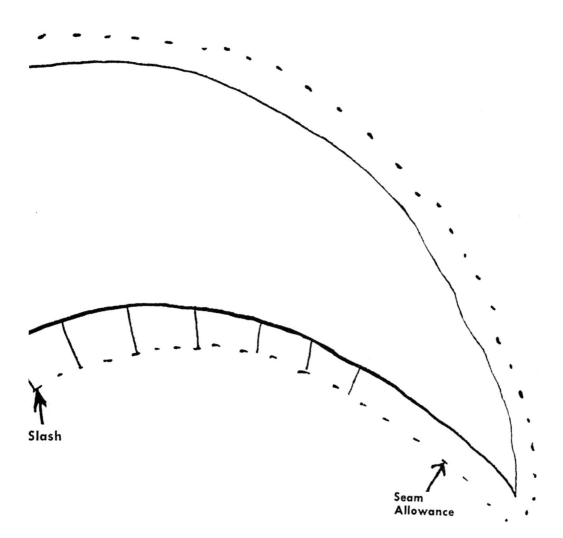

Slash

Seam Allowance

VISOR PATTERN

Figure 49

place in center of bow meeting in back, sew to bow. Sew to hat.

Two loop ribbon bow (figure 50). Use about one yard hat banding or felt, cut ends diagonally. Fold at center. Make flat loop 2½ inches long, pleating *underneath* to center, make another 3¼ inches directly under first, pleating at center back. Extend end out beyond last bow. By folding all loops in the center, make the other half exactly the same, using first bows for measurement. Securely pleat and tack. Pleat one inch piece of ribbon lengthwise and sew forming knot of bow.

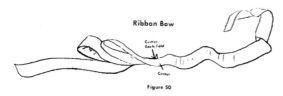

Figure 50

CLOCHE: Block and steam old hat etc. the same as in making calot or jockey. Mark according to hair line and cut one inch below. Trace paper pattern from book (figure 51), and alter brim of pattern if necessary. Use remaining felt or old brim, press out in a complete circle (figure 52), forming a collar around block (figure 53), large enough to fit paper pattern plus ½ inch for hemming inside brim. Place crown on head and put brim *over crown*. Shape and pin into position at an attractive angle (figure 54). This is what is called designing on your head. (Felt may be cut from inside of brim as well as outside.) Ends must meet in center back for cloche style, in straight line. Loosely overcast center back seam (figure 33) and press open and flat. Stitch brim to crown in pinned position with showing stitch (figure 32). Place hat on head block, gently hold back brim and cut ½ inch below, turn under ⅛ inch below where brim meets crown. Lightly press crown edge with iron on block. *Hemming of brim is optional.* A soft brimmed hat does not need hemming.

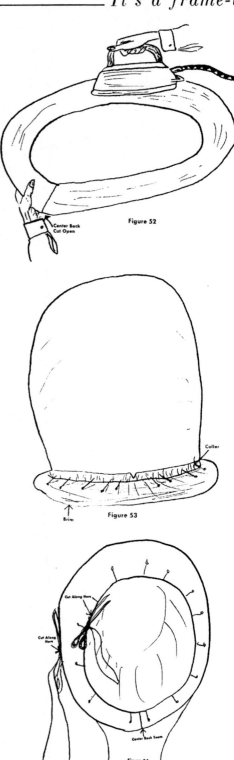

Figure 52

Figure 53

Figure 54

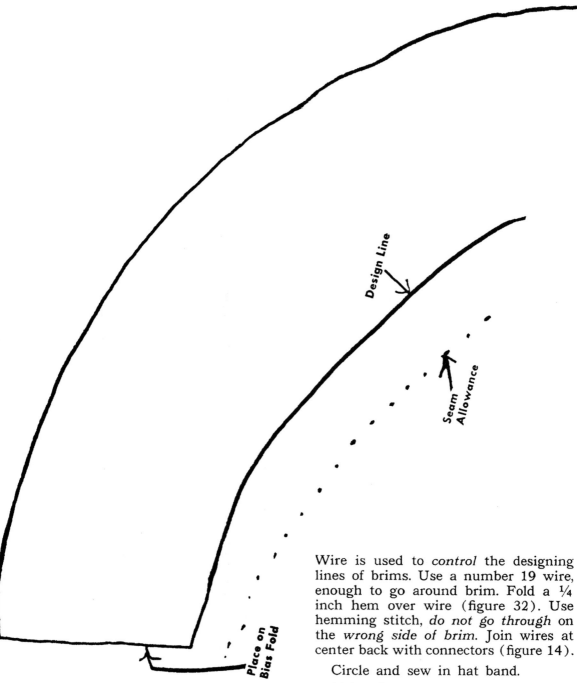

Design Line

Seam Allowance

Place on Bias Fold

PATTERN FOR CLOCHE

Figure 51

Wire is used to *control* the designing lines of brims. Use a number 19 wire, enough to go around brim. Fold a ¼ inch hem over wire (figure 32). Use hemming stitch, *do not go through* on the *wrong side of brim*. Join wires at center back with connectors (figure 14).

Circle and sew in hat band.

Trimming: Cut out narrow strip of felt ¼ inch wide to go around crown and make bow on side or center front. Trim with feather; rose, orchid or veiling if desired.

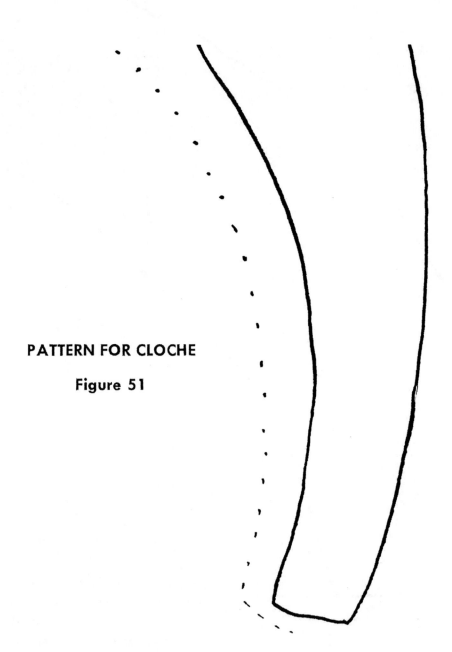

PATTERN FOR CLOCHE

Figure 51

DRAPING FELTS: *Draped crowns:*
For draping a hat it is advisable to steam
and pull the felt to the bottom of the
block removing most wrinkles. This
permits the hat to be raised on the head
block for draping and designing. Design
by pleating (figure 55) and folding
(never overdo) between fingers; pinning
the folds as you go along. After design
has been attained, hold head block in
hand and steam over tea kettle. This
process *permanently sets the folds without tacking.* When thoroughly dry, take
felt off block and try on for effect and
comfort. Fold under excess felt on
desired hair line. Cut off excess seam
allowance inside of crown. Lightly press
final fold line on head block. A plain brim
may be added to any draped crown.
Follow instructions for cloche, but cut
design line right on brim rather than
use a pattern.

Novelty crown draped hat (figure
56). Steam and stretch felt on novelty
block first then place hat on your head
size block before you start to drape the
crown.

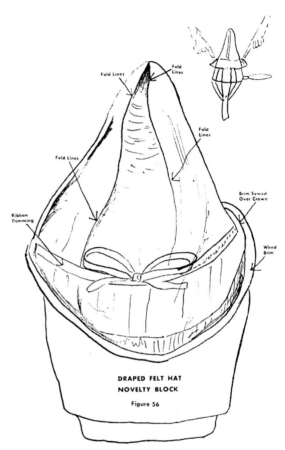

DRAPED FELT HAT
NOVELTY BLOCK

Figure 56

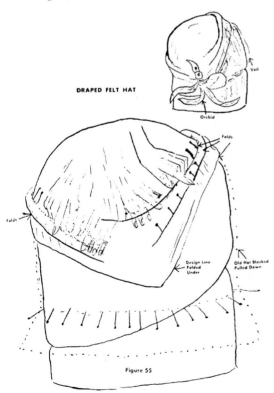

DRAPED FELT HAT

Figure 55

The *plain crown* can be steamed in
shape either on a novelty crown block
or a head size block according to
past directions (figure 2). Measure and
chalk, then cut on hair line.

Press and circle brim (figures 52-
53). Take brim in hands, *stretch* and
drape across and around block in any
design or fold. Sometimes it's easier to
design a hat on your head. Pin in position (figure 57), and permanently set
lines by thoroughly *steaming over tea
kettle.* Completely dry. Remove de-

signed hat from head block, keep well pinned in position. Try on for necessary adjustments. Mark these with chalk or cut with scissors. Any design lines may be changed by *cutting anywhere outside of brim*. Felt brim may also be cut in a design where it *meets the crown*. Hem felt over on wire edge if control for design is necessary. Sew brim to crown with showing stitch. Turn under bottom

edge of crown in an attractive design.

Felt may also be stretched and draped around the block in the same manner as fabric according to directions under draping in relation to frames (figure 30).

Press on fold.

Circle and sew in hat banding.

Final Steam.

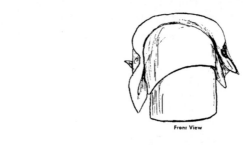

Front View

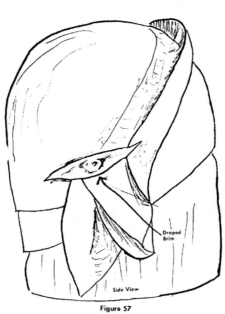

Draped Brim

Side View

Figure 57

STRAWS BRAID STRAW BODIES AND HOODS

There are two kinds of straw, woven and braid. The woven straw is made with one continuous thread, like fabric, such as backu, bali buntle, etc. The braid straws are either interlocking or overlapping braid. The interlocking braid straw has a thread connecting each loop in two rows of braid. The overlapping braid straw has one layer sewed over the other. Straw *can be blocked* and *steamed much the same* way as felt, but I find it easier to lightly press with an iron because of the danger of breaking the threads in the straw by pulling and stretching. If you press the straws with a heavy hand it flattens the braid *too much.* Old straw hats may be restyled. First clean and remove stitches, trimming, and wires. Old straws may be dyed with commercial dyes *after hat is completely restyled.* Braid straws must be unraveled. Remember, you cannot stretch machine stitches; only between the rows of braid. Use braid straw for small hats and a straw body or hood for larger hats (figure 34).

If you are using a new straw body or straw hood, first, you would block the crown; either the press or steam method on the block. The *braid straws would have to be unraveled;* starting and ending in the center back on the design line of the crown. The interlocking braid straw can be separated by cutting the thread between the interlocking loops and pulling the braid apart. The overlapping braids are unraveled by ripping the thread that holds the braid together. You *can* cut the straws on any design line but you would need to wire (if necessary), the outside edges of the brims and bind with ribbon. You can use the outside edges of the braid straw bodies and hoods for the final design line by cutting down the center back of the piece left over from the crown or the brim. 1. Unravel or cut out excess on straw design line. 2. Sew crown to brim. Finish the center back seam or edges according to weight of straw (figure 58).

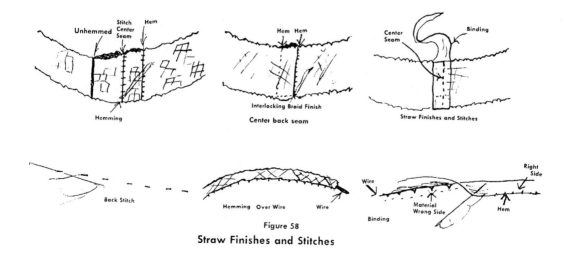

Figure 58
Straw Finishes and Stitches

Sometimes you can make two hats from one straw or felt body, depending on the size of hats.

Sizing: Sizing is a liquid substance somewhat like shellac, used especially for stiffening straws and gives a glossy finish. It should be applied lightly with a brush *to all straws after* the hat is completely designed and finished. Be sure straw is dry. Sizing is *inflammable* and evaporates quickly. It is used to *hold* and not *change* the shape of straws. There is a water white sizing for *all straws* and a milk white for white straws.

Linings are not necessary in straw hats.

Frames as Novelty Blocks: A buckram frame may be used as a pattern and foundation block for the straw braids. Don't sew the straw to the frames, you'll need to lift the frame out from under the straw. If the hat that you want to make has a head size crown, draw line on head block by placing hat on the block then draw design. Take a paper pattern of brim, and follow direction as applied to one of the four basic styles.

PILLBOX: About 2½ yards of one inch braid straw is needed, amount varies according to width of straw and size of pillbox. Braid straw should have same finish on both sides. Use novelty block (figure 35) and saucer of water with sponge to SLIGHTLY wet straw as you progress. Begin at center of crown (figure 59). Wind in a complete circle, never stretching out braid. Place new row of braid just under edge of last row of braid (underlapping). Pin in position as you proceed. Cover top and side with one continuous piece of braid; according to depth desired. Straw should start tapering at side and end

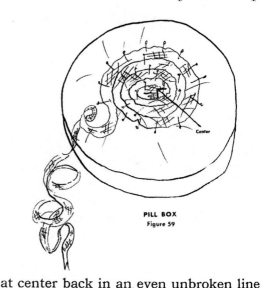

PILL BOX
Figure 59

at center back in an even unbroken line on bottom of hat. Starting at bottom, press *lightly* with iron and cloth, CAUTION — straw burns easily. Also flattens easily. Don't remove pins until thoroughly dry. Remove hat from block, keeping shape intact. Start at center back, sew rows of braid together with invisible back stitch (figure 58).

Circle and sew in hat band.

Size.

Commercial trimmings are suggested for use on straw hats.

WOVEN STRAW-PILLBOX: Select a loosely woven straw body or hood. Slightly wet under faucet, place over novelty block (figure 35), center crown to center block. Stretch evenly and pin to block 3½" down. Sometimes straw must be eased in and pressed flat with iron to fit block. To do this it will be necessary to run a double basting stitch around straw on design line—also around head size and edge of brims. The straw then can be pulled in and up to head size. Mark to desired depth, cut ½" below chalk mark. Fold under on chalk mark, press fold line and top and sides of hat until dry.

Circle and put in hat band.

Size.

STRAW SAILOR

To make a sailor in straw follow the same instructions under felt sailor. The important thing is to have the inside of the brim collar be the same size as the bottom of the crown. Finish the brim as you would under the directions according to the type of straw you're using.

CALOT: Use 2½ yards of one inch wide braid. (figure 60). Working on block with braid, start at center back. Continue around, dampening, pinning and underlapping, same as pillbox. For a design, draw on head block as instructed in felts (figure 46). If design is in *irregular lines,* fill in with extra rows of straw. Or if possible begin gradually on center back of outside line of specially designed calot, having straw

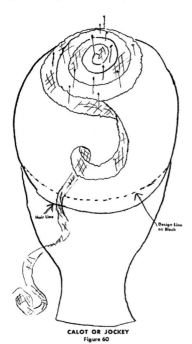

CALOT OR JOCKEY
Figure 60

stitch (figure 58) gaining underneath crown.

Circle and sew in hat band.

Size.

WOVEN CALOT: Use same method for woven straws as pillbox, placing on block in position it is going to be worn. Mark, cut out, or draw irregular design if desired on straw. Allow ½" for turning under. Fold and press on design line.

Circle and sew in hat band.

Size.

JOCKEY: Crown. Read directions for calot. Use four or less yards of one inch wide straw braid with same finish on both sides. With straw slightly damp, start at center of crown on head block, wind, underlap and pin each row as you go along. Fill in with rows of braid to

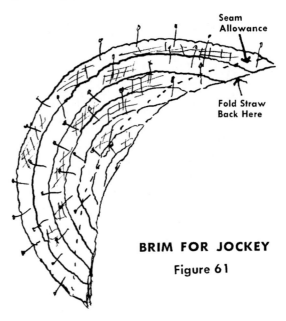

BRIM FOR JOCKEY
Figure 61

end in center of crown or a long line or in any other attractive design. Press and take off to sew, being careful not to lose shape of hat. Sew with back

desired depth of crown. Gage by hair line on block. Remove pins from block and press small section at a time, replace pins in straw so hat can be removed and sew your hat in your hands. Seed back stitch (figure 58).

Brim: Transfer and adjust pattern of brim (figure 49). Trace pattern on padded ironing board with pencil. Mark ½″ seam allowance on inside brim on ironing board. Starting at either point of brim pin slightly dampened straw braid following outside line of brim (figure 61). Turn back straw at opposite side (don't cut off braid) retrace, underlap, damp, and pin as you go along. Continue in preceding manner until pattern is completely filled in. Remove pins on small portion, press and replace pins keeping pattern intact. Sew straw with back stitch, gaining between rows of straw. Stitches show very little on either side. Press a collar against

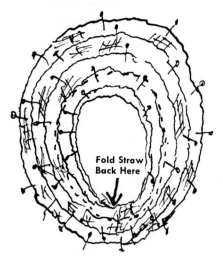

CLOCHE BRIM

Figure 62

block and dry (figure 53). Place brim on crown in desired position with seam allowance under crown.

Circle and sew in hat band. Size hat, to make brim stiffer, size twice. If you desire an extra stiff brim sew an extra row of straw on under side of brim and slip a wire between the two layers of straw.

CLOCHE: Crown is made like jockey filling in with straw braid in a circle to hair line on block. For brim, use paper pattern, fit and trace on padded ironing board. Allow ½″ on inside of brim. Following outside edge, start at center back, dampen, underlap, and pin until brim and seam allowance is filled in (figure 62). Sew with back stitch. Form collar against head block inside brim (figure 53). This fits inside on crown and gives something to sew crown to. Place crown on head. Pin and fit brim into attractive position. Place back on head block and chalk mark where brim meets crown. Fold ½″ below chalk line inside crown; and cut off excess straw. Place crown over brim. Center back of brim vertically joining center back of crown. Sew with back stitch. Circle and sew in hat band. Lightly size hat. For a stiffer brim, size brim again. Wire may be strung in ribbon or velvet hat tubing for an extra stiff brim. Sew tubing to either top or bottom edge of brim. Connect wires with joiners at center back. (Figure 14).

WOVEN CLOCHE: Block crown same as jockey, following hair line. In tracing brim pattern allow 3/8 inch for hemming over a number 19 wire on edge of brim. Use a joiner at center back (figure 14). Join straw at center back with flat hemming (figure 58).

HOW TO MAKE A FRAME

Very often the style or fit of a frame wanted is not available, so it is necessary to make your own. It is much easier to buy a frame ready made because you can be sure of the fit and design, but when the proper style and size is not at hand, knowing how to make your own frame is important.

Buckram and wire is used to form and control the lines of the frames. Crinoline is used to cover the rough edges, and flexo for a soft flexible line. Organdy or lining may be substituted for crinoline. The important thing is to be very careful about making your frame too stiff and severe.

PILLBOX: To make a pillbox copy a pillbox by using the paper pattern method or by making a paper pattern of a circle which is the desired width, never larger than the head size. This means a range from 6½ to 8 inches in diameter. Materials needed are ½ yard of buckram and 1½ yards of number 19 wire. Trace paper pattern on true bias of buckram and allow ¼ inch for seams. Clip buckram with scissors up to style line and fold down seam allowance (figure 10). Cut a 2½" strip of bias the same length as the circumference of the crown and allow one inch at each end for overlapping at center

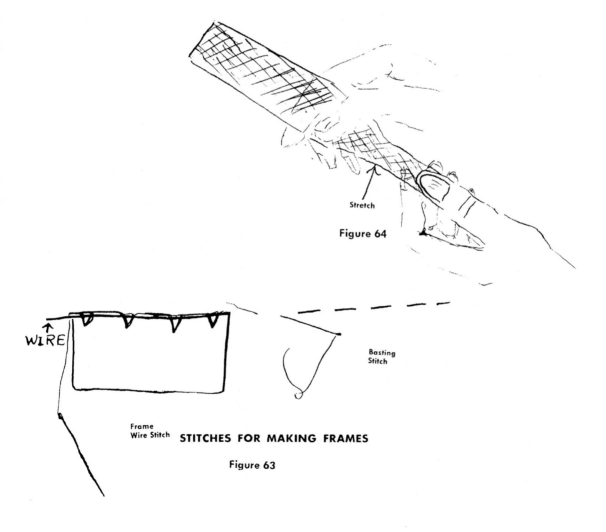

Stretch

Figure 64

WIRE

Basting Stitch

Frame
Wire Stitch **STITCHES FOR MAKING FRAMES**

Figure 63

back seam. Sew seam together at back. No other seam allowance is needed on top or bottom of side crown. Use the same length of wire, No. 19, as side crown piece of buckram. Sew wire to edge of side crown with frame wire stitch (figure 63). (Almost like a blanket stitch. This is the strongest stitch in millinery.) Overlap wire at center back. Also sew wire at bottom side of crown, overlapping at center back. This forms a brace. To cover wire and rough edges at bottom, cut one inch strip of crinoline on true bias same length as side crown piece. Gently stretch crinoline between fingers (figure 64). This stretching enables the crinoline to fall smoothly into the curves of the hat. Fold crinoline in half and place half on inside and the remaining half on outside, bottom of side crown, overlapping at back. Sew with basting stitch. Also sew crinoline to top side of crown. Place crown on side crown with clipped segments inside and sew crowns together with overcasting stitch keeping true circle.

CALOT: Use a 12 inch square of completely wet buckram, place over top of block. Pull and stretch; pin vertically. Remove all wrinkles above hair line mark.

The same square may be placed on a block and steamed over a tea kettle as explained previously under lining (figures 15-16-17). Also, buckram may be pressed with iron and wet cloth on a block. (See lining directions.)

Draw any desired design following instruction under felt calot. Cut one inch below design and try on. Fold up along design and make any desired changes. Cut off excess buckram at finish design line. Complete bottom edge of buckram in calot same as bottom edge of pillbox, with wire and crinoline.

JOCKEY: Either steam, wet, or press a 12 inch square over block, stretching or pulling out all wrinkles above hair line. Cut off at hair line. Mark center back and center front. To remove from block, run flexible, flat, narrow knife underneath buckram. Fold up excess buckram according to personal fit and depth. Cut off smoothly on fold. Wire and cover crown with crinoline as stated under pillbox.

BRIM: Trace pattern and cut on bias of buckram. Clip inside seam allowance and fold back segments to seam line. Wire outside edge of brim and sew with wire stitch (figure 63). Cover with crinoline and sew. I suggest that the crown and brim be covered first with material according to directions under jockey before attaching brim to crown. After covering, pin brim to crown, placing seam allowance inside crown and sew.

CLOCHE: Use a 12 inch square of buckram and block crown similar to that of jockey but cut one inch below hair line. Mark center back and center front. Remove from block and place on head for fit. To make brim, transfer pattern on newspaper. With crown still on head, place brim pattern around and adjust for attractiveness. Pin pattern in position; overlap paper at center back. Mark with pencil where brim meets crown. Cut off crown smoothly, on pencil line. Finish edge of crown according to past direction under pillbox. Cut out paper pattern of brim on buckram, center front on true bias. Allow for seams on inside line of brim, plus enough for one inch overlap at center back. Clip inside circle up to pattern line and fold segments up. Overlap and sew center back together. Finish outside edge of brim by wiring and covering as stated under pillbox. Suggest covering crown and brim separately with material, following direction under cloche frame; then place crown over brim with seam allowance inside of crown.

COVER ORIGINAL

Make or purchase tubing (Piquet or velvet) 1½ yards long. String number 20 inch wire same length through tubing. Connect wires with joiner (figure 14) clamp tightly with pinchers. Sew ends of velvet together at point where wire connects, leave thread attached. Form a complete circle (figure 66). Use connecting point for center back; therefore center front is directly across cluster front. Place center front on center front of head two inches back of hair line. Follow contour of head and bend wire at right angles at ears. Continue with wire to center back of head on hair line at neck. Cross wires at hair line at center back. Bring up center back to crossed wires forming a bow (figure 67). Sew securely together by wrapping needle and thread around wires. Loops should be identical on each side. Find outside center of loop and bend to form a butterfly wing (almost to center back). Fold other side the same way. Sew on groups of flowers. (Possibly one flat rose with two sprays on each side. Use any combination of flowers; don't

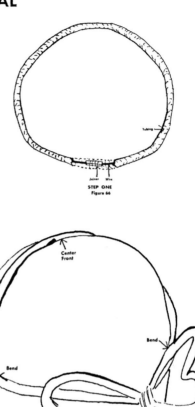

STEP ONE
Figure 66

FOUNDATION
Figure 67

skimp. Amount and quality of flowers determines the quality of the hat.) Flowers should be sewed to butterfly loop. Place on head, bend wire forward to contour of neck in back of head. Use one yard of narrow veiling 2½ to 4 inches wide. Find center of veiling and place in center of face. Drape veiling across eyes; don't rub eyelashes, then gather slightly and tack to right angle at bend above ears. Bring each end of remaining veiling to center back covering top half of flowers. Cut off excess ends and sew.

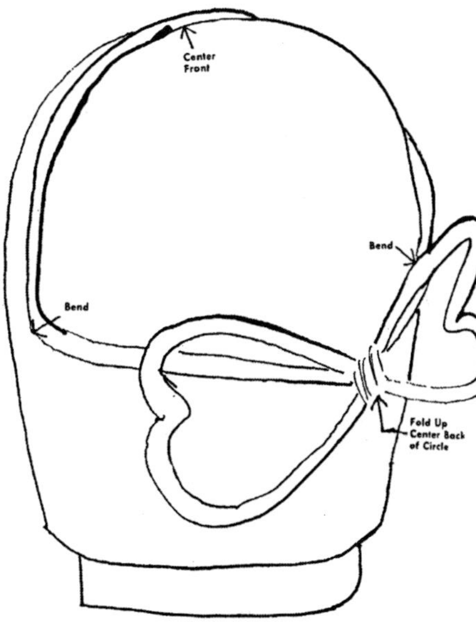

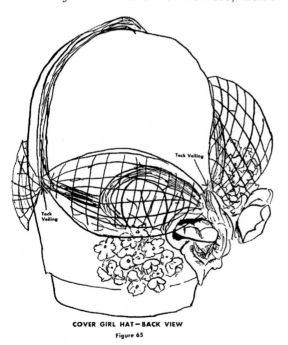

COVER GIRL HAT – BACK VIEW
Figure 65

SPECIAL DESIGN

Purchase a bicycle clamp. Use velvet ribbon or hat banding wide and long enough to cover bicycle clamp. Sew outside edge on machine and slip in bicycle clamp. Arrange flowers, real or commercial in a spray about 18 inches long (must extend over clamp). To make veiling use ¾ yards of soft complexion veiling 18 inches wide. Sew 12 inches of narrow velvet ribbon to each end of tightly gathered veil. Tack center of veiling to center of wreath and 1½ inches beyond each side. Take ribbon end of veiling and drape veil over face, tie in back of your head.

SPECIAL DESIGN

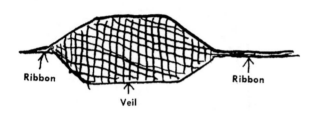

Ribbon   Ribbon

Veil

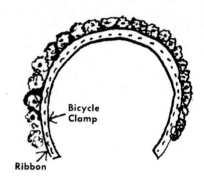

Bicycle
Clamp

Ribbon

HOW TO COPY A HAT

When copying a hat (figure 68), take the paper pattern of a hat following the same principle of taking a paper pattern from a frame and applying the principles according to directions under the kind of fabric, felt or straw, you are using. In copying the hat pictured above (figure 68), pin and fit the paper pattern to the brim only. Suggest drawing the lines of crown with pencil on head block or frame itself. (It might be necessary to make own frame, which is a calot.) Use lines as guide lines for seams for draping material and follow directions for sectional crown if using fabric. Finish brim and crown according to directions for felt, straw, or fabric, whichever you are using. I suggest that you make a one piece crown in felt or straw. Fit brim on outside of crown, except small section marked on dotted line below dart, which goes inside of crown. The complete pattern for brim and sectional crown is given in figure 69.

Trimming: Wire a string of pearls and place along outside edge of brim. Lightly sew on outside. Also, a narrow spray of tiny flowers may be used along edge of brim.

For felt or fabric, the brim could be a solid color (blue) on the outside and a pale color (white) on the inside. The outside edge of brim must be hemmed over a wire; use the showing stitch for felt and woven straw, and the finished wire stitch for fabric.

In braid straw, string wire in velvet tubing and sew to outside edge of brim. Twist flap in circle and let come forward on crown. This can be twisted higher to give the illusion of height.

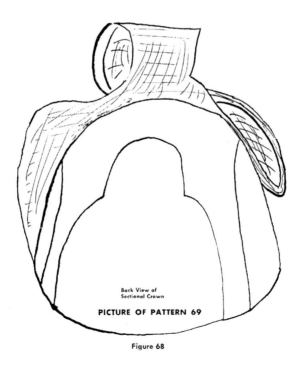

Back View of
Sectional Crown

PICTURE OF PATTERN 69

Figure 68

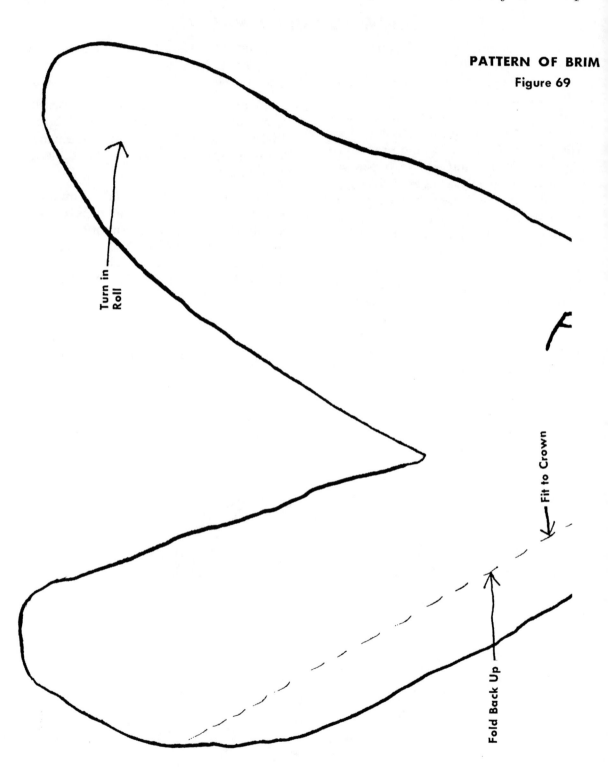

PATTERN OF BRIM
Figure 69

Turn in Roll

Fit to Crown

Fold Back Up

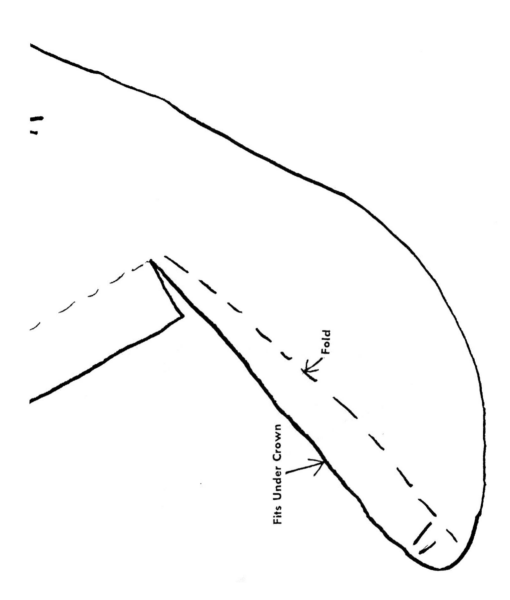

PATTERN OF BRIM

Figure 69

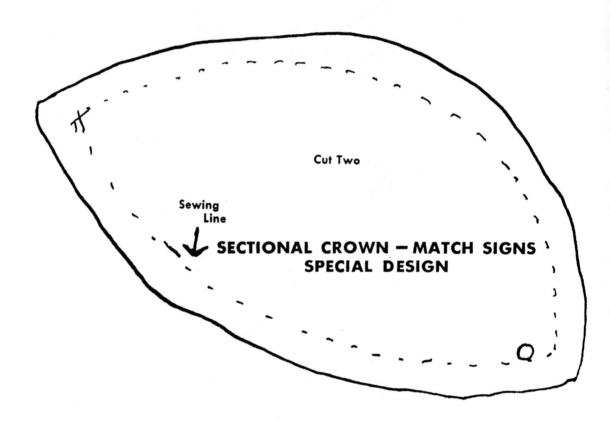

Cut Two

Sewing
Line

**SECTIONAL CROWN – MATCH SIGNS
SPECIAL DESIGN**

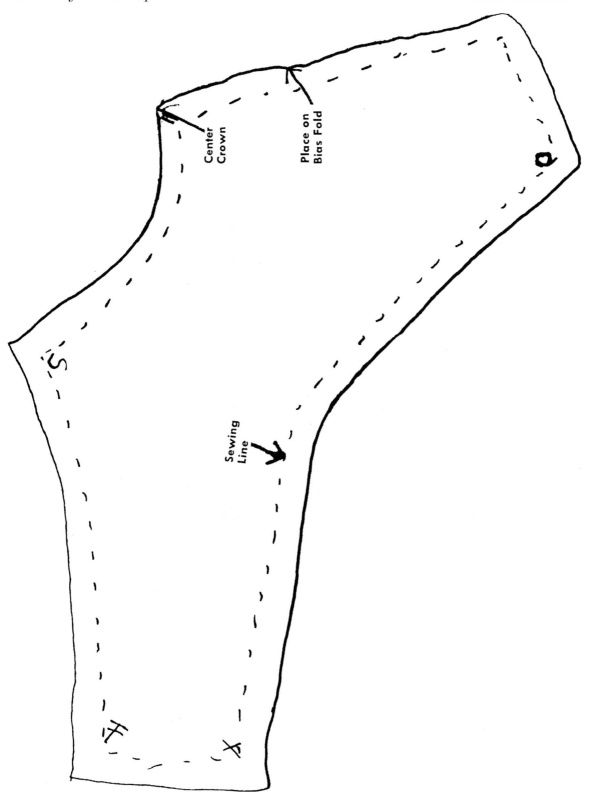

Center
Crown

Place on
Bias Fold

Sewing
Line

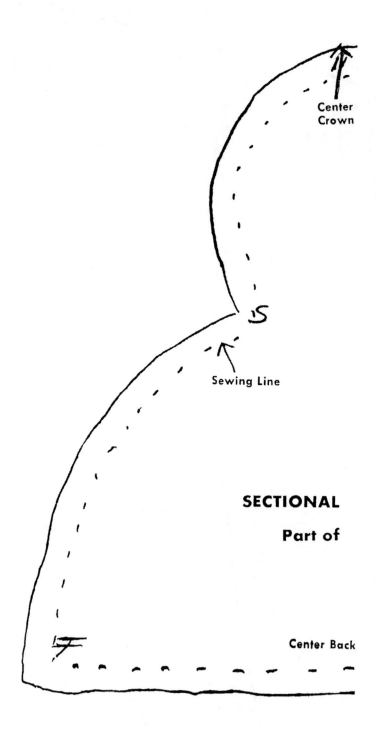

Center
Crown

Sewing Line

SECTIONAL

Part of

Center Back

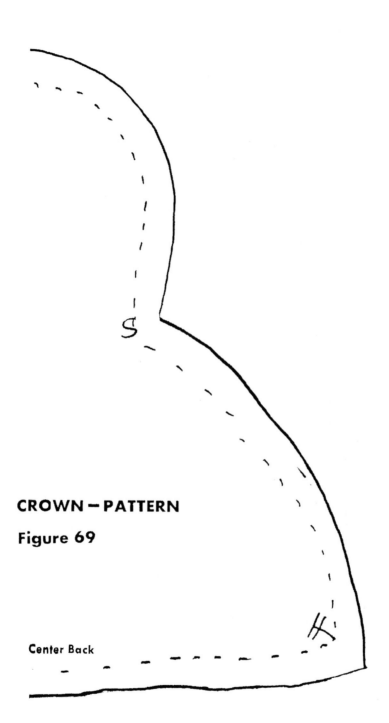

CROWN – PATTERN

Figure 69

Center Back

FUR

Fur may be used on a fabric covered frame hat or a felt hat. By taking a paper pattern of the brim or crown where you can determine just how much fur is needed. Suggest you take the pattern to your furrier before you buy too much fur. Trace outlines of paper pattern of brim on ironing board; allow ¼ inch for seams. *Skin may be slightly dampened and stretched to fit any curve of a block or paper pattern*. Pin or nail fur to ironing board until dry. Place fur side down, being sure fur runs in same direction, usually down (figure 70). To make fur fit pattern, lightly cut skin with razor

blade. Do not cut through to fur because hair must overlap on outside. Separate skin from fur by lightly pulling apart. Put fur sides together and tightly overcast skins; seams should not show on right side. Sew together as many pieces as are necessary to fill in paper pattern. Use cotton twill or skirt tape on outside of design line tightly overcast by putting tape on fur side and push back fur and sew tape to skin around edges of brim. Fold tape and fur over ⅛ inch to wrong side (enough to hide tape). Slip stitch to skin. Fur is finished; slip stitch directly to finished brim.

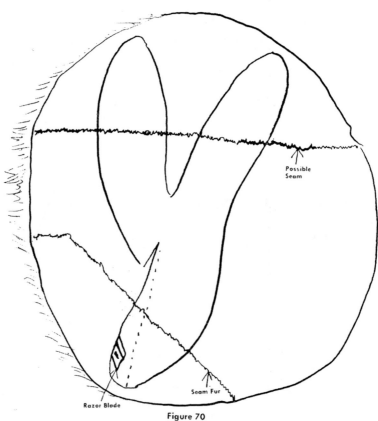

Figure 70

CUTTING FUR FROM PATTERN

HAT MADE FROM TIES

Hats made from ties are attractive because the fabric is usually so colorful. They can be worn all year around, and can perk up a basic dress. Several hats can be made for just the cost of a frame if discarded ties are used. Although you can use one of the four basic frames, use an outstanding frame—to bring out the varied, colorful design—or two contrasting colors may be used.

To make, select a tie with an overall pattern. Rip out all seams; either dry clean or wash. Sometimes inside is brighter than right side of tie — use whichever looks best. Sometimes it is easier to stretch and drape tie material over the frame by following the lines of the frame than using a paper pattern. To make sectional crown, follow the lines of frame for design or calot directions. Drape brim and crown separately. Circle and sew in hat banding; line according to previous directions.

The hat pictured on the back cover is made in a two section calot crown. The stitch up section is taken off the crown and made in two pieces (one inside and one outside). The outside piece is completed with a wire finish, same as the cloche brim.

ALL OVER FLOWERED HATS

When you make a flowered hat remember that flowers are bulky and you should choose a small foundation.

The commercial foundations are made of different colored rice net. They come already designed and do not need any other fabric covering or a lining. The edges are usually bound with ribbon and need no other hat banding. You can make your own frame by blocking a 12″ square of rice net or buckram on a block by following the directions under making frames.

If you use a buckram frame you will need to completely cover smoothly the frame first. Use either lining material or French crepe, or organdy.

Flowers and leaves should be glued directly on frame. Not at all necessary to *SEW* flowers on frame. Flowers can be placed all over the foundation or worked in an attractive design. Use flowers singularly or in little bunches. Little velvet ribbon bows placed between the flowers are an added attraction.

Sequins pasted on the flower petals are very attractive (or sew individual jewels to the petals).

Stretch fine veiling or net over the whole hat for added protection of the flowers. You can make your own flowers and stems by brushing straw sizing on velvet or any fabric; two coats if necessary. Cut out a small flower design (any variety of flowers). The sizing makes the velvet very stiff and the flowers will not ravel after being cut out. Buy little yellow tips for centers or use little yellow discs of velvet.

Make strips of ribbon by sizing material (Taffeta or velvet) and cut up in desired width.

Dyeing Trimmings: To dye flowers; thoroughly mix a few daubs of paint of any desired shade from a small tube of oil paint into one quart of most any dry cleaning fluid. Dip flowers, feathers, or ribbon and some straws in quickly and dry. Keep turning the trimmings over on a towel until dry. Dip again for darker shades.

INDEX

Don't throw money away! Turn old material you have in your own home into beautiful, stylish new hats by using . . . **OLD FELT, OLD FUR AND FEATHERS, THAT OUT-MODED STRAW OR FELT, NECKTIES, FLOWERS OR SUITING.**

This new book shows you how simple it is to make your own hats to suit your personality.

LaVergne, TN USA
17 May 2010
182745LV00004B/3/P